24

All rights reserved. No part of this book may be reproduced
or transmitted in any manner, without prior permission
by the publisher, except for reviewers who may quote brief passages.

Printed with the support of the Alkion Press Fund

ISBN- 978-1-7340170-8-3

Copyright © 2021 Leif Garbisch

First Edition

Printed in the USA

Published in 2021
by Alkion Press
14 Old Wagon Road, Ghent, NY 12075

Title: 24
Author: Leif Garbisch
Cover: Leif Garbisch

24

POEMS

LEIF GARBISCH

Contents

Young Life With Sun 7
For 10
One December 11
Incarnate 12
Resolve 14
Growing Thoughts 16
For Everything Included 18
River 19
This Place This Moment 22
Insight 23
All Ours 24
Charmed Life 25
Thought The Morning 27
Becoming Love .28
Cloud Rider 29
Seeing Without Device 30
Lift 33
Learning To See .34
Longing For Space 36
After A Long Rain 37
The Nature Of Light 38
The Soul Tree 39
The Chance To Be Visible 40
The Change 42

Young Life With Sun

My mother sits at the table. There are no ghosts
no bottle of wine. Her hands are dirty from work. She has always
looked in upon me and forward to where I'm going. My father appears
through the window, arrives through the front door, says something
I cannot make out, then something I can, sees me
by the back door ready to go, and I know
he, too, craves this life. And my mother, green like the birch
buds becoming leaves soon, sun coming in low now, hands now
on the table, cutting the sheen, opening. Seeds that need planting,
soil in pots. She says to him tomato. He says carrot to her, corn.
He says beautiful he says to her day. His face says the light and will say it
long into the night. I have nothing to add at this moment, nothing much
to give back, not as I am, young with no innovative plot, no
intriguing self to put into words, into the world, except to say
that I spent the days of my childhood blindly studying. The sun
steadied my body against the wind, which buffeted me about. I was
stirred by wind and light. And then at night a deep and peace
full sleep. So –   Bye, I say. Good-bye. And they
say Good-bye back my way, bright and bold, because they wish
to appear unafraid. I won't be gone longer than they can foresee, will
find my place, no doubt come home. And as I swing the door wide the wide
opening door sings that same hinge song it has squealed before, asks how far
I'm planning to go, asks how soon until I return, worries

about me like my fear-masking parents, and like any good door
loves to make way for
                                        So many questions. I
don't always know the answers, but I like to think I do. There is time
to figure and test, with acres in front, earth and sky
and a wake that spreads so far behind I might never find its source,
as if I've come from some illimitable place, love it is, liquid
and've been living on water ever since – my days as a boat
cutting through, and the wake that secures me to some origin anticipates
somewhere new, like a V of geese that points to green welcoming fields. And warm
it is, late this good day, Friday by the calendar, spring sun setting here in the hills,
the freshening earth, returning birds. And I, too, thirst
waiting for my friend to pick me up. No, not up up. I'm
already there. High among. Calm before the storm. Not wanting
beer or routine thought but more of that water I mentioned. And no fatigue
but good fatigue. No flowers I can now see. I don't need flowers to see. I don't want
different eyes, either. I don't want any other mind or soul or time or lay
of life. I want what I've got the way it is mine, in my face and at my feet
and through my hair the wind, and toward my tongue a word. It grows
inside me. Expression spills out, it ripples my body as if I am also
water, as if I'm days I'm boat I'm liquid I'm love, and what I say
catches the light, and it morphs the trees in the changing sky
and loosens the colors so they, too, can think on their own, so they, too
can grow in this world and stand true with each other – deepening blue calling
out blue, softening orange ready to go, the red brake lights, the bright
of the car turning silver, turning round slow, the sound of the engine and the rock

of the road, rocks on the road, and me getting in, closing the door
and driving off.
                                      I'm leaving my home
leaning into the curve and curving west where the sun
a while ago full of work and wishes went, full of will to give – it went
of warmth and days and years to come – that sun. It is no longer apparent
light now, it is hands now, upon my denim legs and in my breast, throughout.
Good sun now teaming within, now straightening out now
going forth from the ever-present first, from every beginning
from love now from now now and far
far into my proof that here at last
I am and thanks
and thanks to all, I start from here
moving into sight

For

the living who know little of the dead, for the dead
who sit in the back seat listening, for the whole
of life that remains unknown, for the earth
that stands by, awaiting our commitment
out of chaos morass bondage.   I am free
to think and act. With the setting sun I'm able
to chat, with the shallow waters to listen better, quiet
breeze on the leaves of the dappled marsh grasses.
And these cool sands shift, I'm at sea no longer.
The wind is light the air is light this shell light, too
that I've picked from the shore. I may lift it and see
may feel the weight of each elemental other. The driftiest
wood, the dry beach grains, the suddenly visible spirit
loose alongside those bursting seedheads
when I least expect it.
                                        Thank you, I say.
For the flourishing world the dying-down wind the wash
of waves and cries of gulls, for creation that's wholly
present on earth, for the light in my heart, for the heart
of evening light that holds me, never diminishing
I now speak. Up to the sky, out to the world
with and how, how not, ever and always

One December

One night a knock came to my door
I swung it wide, and what's more
the person standing cold outside
disappeared before my eyes.
Now, what a shock it was. How strange.
But I've seen it happen when it rains
that empty holes will disappear
and puddles soon be everywhere.
How they got there, I don't know.
I think it's due to Christmas, though.
For one December in the woods
walking without gloves or hood
knowing exactly where I was
I stopped near midnight, trees above
the brightness of the wind
through everything
and all I felt was love

INCARNATE

You are here. In the morning weather. Near
the fallen tree, getting wet. The only way
to make a real difference is to become
someone new you are not. That is
what this world asks of you
when you are born. You come again
to a body a home another evolution, slow
reunion with earth. The storm you hear, the rain
dripping from the leaves, spilling upon
the ground, illuminates you. You glisten
like the foliage beside the stream. There's this
broken tree so you can touch its bark, and love
begins to grow the way life intends. Don't take it
from me. Ask for yourself. Life says: "Yes.
I do intend. But you can have your own way
of thinking. Harvest wood, build connections
see another point of view. I met a woman once,"
says life, "whose children were trees, cousins
the clouds. Goes to show, you can hold all
my family in your heart your mind your
soul, astonishing stars. You are this
universe, dark space with light, traveling through,
and what you understand today is larger
than yesterday. You're a door swung wide

to what's out there, and the rain is sometimes
in your face. The sharpness of the morning
storm makes you turn away, and that's okay
because though you might falter, though its push
is ferocious, you can't give up on the earth for long.
You return to it. You lean in. The wind and you
work together, and wherever you are you are
here for something. Not for me to say. Soaking
up the world, its offerings coming at you, the gleam
of being, becoming someone never before seen

Resolve

Wind wind wind wind coming wind in coming
though the
                    places wind comes from, comes
through the
                    leaves, leaves me believing, oak
leaves and grasses and
                          How long's it been since –
the last time I had it was when the rain
ran mud rivers down the road, brought
me out, covered me with wet. The tickling
water down my face. The wind back then
picked up and I got it, got all it had borne, it
introduced itself and
                            Everyone says the world is hard
work now – summertime but cooler with this breeze. Sun
comes out from behind the clouds, the wind
like a guide to me blows clean through
my clothes my body my soul these fields
and trees, and here I am rocked, more
ready than not, standing in increasing
stillness that all I can feel is filling within
and all I can think is that my every
thought readies me here, steadies
my way and wells with life.

It's not what I'm trying
to do. It's – you
                 I now know. Such spirit
as speaks – my ageless ennobler, my endless
reminder, mines that are deep
and what treasures I find
the store of myself, the hoard
of time, hours more hours
to give. This
winded awakening relentlessly world.
What greater miracle than that
I may love. To work here
to bring you home
to the family to say
you within, to say you
without question
                 I will rule now
reign, never quit quite, never
quiet either, neither
come undone

GROWING THOUGHTS

Sun up sun down stars out cars
on the road beams of light in the distance
the black shapes of trees against the night sky. What if
that's all the meaning we get? End of winter. Sure is quiet.
I can hear the dandelions just wishing to grow. I can feel
the shadows move, can, if I concentrate, see the light
the earth lives in. Light – just on the other side
of that hill. The other side of the earth. I'm pointing
through the stone the mantle the core. My heart
seizes the depth of light, hears its stories
knows its truth.
                    In truth, I head off. From the shore
my boat goes. Sea to get across. What is it I'm after?
You know what it is, love. I watch I rock I rise subside.
The most beautiful reason the black waters fall upon. The
openest ocean. I'm getting near. Clearer, I mean. Starry
as this sky. I've lost all consternation, found
a consecration of the world around. I
make my way, a mind without burdens
the loosest of bodies.
                          Understanding you is easy
enlightening, life. Fast as ice melting in a fire of. Ah,
that's meaning for you. A puddle a sizzle.
What changes becomes. If that's not a door

it's a key. If not a key, a clue. Like a hint of spring, of
summer, too. Imagine it. Yellow flowers, bees, honey
sweet air.   I take in
what I meet as seeds that wash my soul, that wake
in me a charge – an earth of hope. I breathe for reasons
all around, as all around breathes me. We live
this reciprocity. All I grow I give

For Everything Included

The universe, large as it is, gives humble clues, limited
stars, never enough comfort to the weary. Somewhere else
there is a bigger picture. Down by the old cottonwood
where first we met. Remember it? A visit

from the sun unhidden after so much
night. We listened for light among the upper limbs.
Why, you asked, are we here in this unfathomable
day, ever at odds with one another? The wind

blew through the winter branches, the trickle of a half
frozen stream. For everything included. For welcoming
love into life, this opening heart. No more fighting
in what you think and do. The sound a truck makes

heading to work. For that deer, you see, looking long at us

River

We woke early, got on the boat, and went
down river, towards the sun. The sun asked
to ride along, and we made room in the bow.

It was hot with the orb, but the autumn air
cooled us so all was good. The sun, typical,
kept asking questions. One – What's your favorite

drink? Lemonade, water, coffee, beer. And
how about your favorite weather? Sunny, of course.
Low humidity. Seventy degrees. Honey bees

butterflies out and about. And the wind light enough
to pass by without shoving. The sun laughed at the thought
of wind that loves. Shoves, we corrected. The river waves lapped

at the hull of our boat. And we came to a bridge and under,
in the deep shadows, sat a group of homeless
adults, children. Seven stray dogs, cats. Four shopping carts

filled with blankets, bottles, broken clocks from town.
I know them all, said the sun. I'll stay here a while. Really nice
traveling with you, though. Let's do this again. And the sun

shone off as we continued beyond the bridge, drifting
with the current, looking ahead to the ocean, or what we assumed
would be the ocean. Late afternoon we turned to check back

on the sun. The water behind us sparkled. The sun had come
apart. Pieces of it lay scattered on the river. We passed the beautiful
glints from mind to mind, and breathed the brightness

of the day. Trees on the banks shed leaves, like tears. The water bore
the burden. It was autumn, and we felt melancholic without the whole
sun, a world in trouble, torn world, idiotic. And why not uplifting

instead. We were angry, not knowing. Sad, not knowing why. What if
we were to wake tomorrow and the river. Was. Just. Gone. What if
our favorite feeling to live with was fear, and our favorite time, what if

it was the end of light? Insane, right? The true sun behind us steadily
settled. We listened for it, red slow brilliant, back with the homeless
at the bridge, listened for it among the all falling orange leaves. We

leaned and listened. The waves of the river lapped again and again
against our boat. Sometimes we choose to pay attention. Other times
we open our hands like baskets full of worries, questions. So, what

is the absolute best decision we've ever made? someone asked.
What do we as human beings do better than trees? We go
to the world like the sun, said another. We pass love

among ourselves the way the wind passes by. Some of us
nodded. Maybe we felt the change in our world, the sun
gone down, the first of all stars. And then the moon rose

in front, over the endless river, speaking from some
perpetual source. We took in the words, reflecting upon
the passage of love. And we proceeded with our floating because

because in our flow – all of life. In our hearts – the rudder, and
above us the stars becoming bright becoming lush
in the wide woven hushness of our moving on

THIS PLACE THIS MOMENT

This morning, early, I stood without symbols, the sun
in my eyes breaking above the horizon made light of me.
Thanks, I said, though I knew it wasn't listening. Lots
to do with spring coming on. When I turned to leave
I saw a fox by the still frozen pond, the sun on her fur,
not far from home. The world is more trustworthy than you know.
I have felt its welcoming touch from the scratch
of a branch, in the glistening wind, upon the moist melt
of snow. Without this place we would not be able
to meet at a distance. To accept each other.
And then it was gone, that animate moment
whose home not far stood shy inside, light
as I was learning to be, brighter by the minute
as if a door opening might change my life

INSIGHT

To the unremembered people
who paved the way
for an illuminated world
and are now gone – how
am I to thank you?
Your desire for truth
had no bounds, and so
when I turn inward, when
I look out upon
a troubled earth
overwhelmed by uncertainty
I see light
an infinite friend
talking to the dark
and the dark forever
opens its hands
and within this
openness – all
that is hidden

All Ours

All ours the day the night
the puddles on pavements
the fields and cows. Ours
the farm and farmer, the framework
of societies, society of stars, laws
for speeding and the speed
of light.   There comes

a moment, just out of the woods
into the open, when…   Then it's gone
so fast. The family of existence
torn apart, turns away, recedes as a dream,
gives me room to remember on my own.   I do not
own the room or anything in it, nor do you.   Wrens
own nothing, not even their nests in the eaves, their flight
through the sky.   All ours of life for life by

the side of the road where the blue flowers grow
links us, inescapably. We are
born to be a family. Birds gradually
come near

Charmed Life

I am mesmerized looking
out of sight here in the meadow, the web
of life, white clouds drifting by. And lo
the windblown leaves sent to hypnotize
my mind my soul, I take by the hand
instead.   There is beauty
all around – bright unhidden things
to transfix my attention. Dim spiritual links
and a rippling pond to captivate me. And yet
the connecteder I am, the furtherer I'm free. It's just
as Lewis Carroll might've said. At least
it's something to think about, to work at –
freedom, as the sun does it
around the clock, shedding light
on the earth, and how the stars navigate
all through the night, or the way swifts fly
tirelessly upon the sky, and truckers
haul, hardly resting, down the road. I spend
my time so I may work to see
to better and to be with each of you, world
no matter the wear on my body, no matter
the attendance needed, or the snow
I've got to shovel so to clear the path, or the hot
humid summers when I'm dripping with sweat

when the shade's just so nice.   O
give me a moment   I'll return the gift.
Give me a minute   I'll turn it into years.
The lovinger I live, the truthfuler I'm here

Thought The Morning

A fine line a forming thought – the morning
sun through the window wakes my heart
with its nearness that if only I could
do the same and why not live as light

in the world, the leaf gleam and puddles
spark my interest in the surface feast and more
the heights of human reach. O turtle, Issa
didn't write – climb bearing the earth, move

closer to life

Note: The poet Kobayashi Issa wrote a haiku
of a snail climbing Mount Fuji, very slowly.

BECOMING LOVE

I am built of everyone's stories.
I am but a house of I's. Or
is. I – living words. Strong measured
wind knocks at my door. Late
breaking waves upon the shoreline. Tides
leave gifts I meet each hour. The hum
of earth and purl of water. Read it aloud –
I'm made of this life. Am walks
at night the dark and moonless, out
the stars that look my way, deep into
my warp and woof, spark
of fireflies, ache of ice. For I
am built of light and shadows
morning sun that filters through the trees
the plots of foxes, owls, and flowers, the
griefs and growths of every person. Other
I's shape the humble me. The more
the open gate I'm all things, more
the law is love becoming

Cloud Rider

Receive me O
earth I
rain
as if glistening
love upon fields
tilled by day
and sowed
by night – I
compose doors
each season
mend exits
for years
seep deep
speak up
grow us
out of absence
into all

Seeing Without Device

      ...on this, the third day of rain,
I caught a glimpse. In the gray green summer
late afternoon, pooled with glistening clues. I
put down my camera to better
take hold
              I don't need beauty
arranged in puddles on the gleaming pavement
or as silver droplets on seven black branches. I do
need to remember it as the root of all being – that
entering a closeness makes what's beautiful
possible to know
                           How unafraid I am
of life. I look at the street outside, glazed
with rainwater – the trees people the place
saturated with meaning, so much
that I'm completely absorbed.
I've come to the world again
and again, eyes opening
at birth. I've allowed all forms all
light to teach me, and the reach
of my involvement has roved wide, been long
ringing out
              Bells in the distance, wind
through the maple leaves, voices

I hear when the world has the chance
to speak
           To me, it says – Here is the picture.
A drop of rain on a mirror lake. You
do not stop at this brief moment
on earth. There is more life to get to,
this door then the next, ever greater
circles of inclusion. And the grasses
wave, they root for you. The clouds are
your biggest fans. Hidden sun and moon, too.
All shades of blue, of red, what wet green hues
grow in the fields, what music is composed
by the dripping eaves, and what joy it is
after a long liquid day taking pictures
to be home, dry feet, at ease
with someone, a softness to her
step, the faint sound of boiling
water
                        Together
this night. I expose my heart and the sky
inside lives, never to be forgotten, gaining
light, growing family. Stars appear. I open
my eyes to their way of seeing the world
from a spiritual perspective. They celebrate
our place in the universe, rainy weather and all
fresh thoughts, each birth and death,

every color and voice, our sleep and mostly
when we awake. The stars stay up late
reflecting on our connections. They see
from afar what I see close by. They
listen to what I have to say. So,
I put away my camera and see
without device. Life is pleased
to be clear
            all my words wish
                        to usher in love

LIFT

Lift – unloosen – hand on life
heart more true each hour
to see the light that is my self
sun alike no other

To be and yes to answer things
within without a fear
always moving closer yet
unto the possibler

Extend – unfolding – to what end
wind in flowers, wheeling stars
they work their awe that I might grow
down the road the world my door

Learning To See

Without the light inside I would not see. You
would not see me. The leaves that are lit would
be lit for no one. With light inside I
hardly need the sun, though it's nice
waking in the morning and everywhere
I look and wherever I walk, what
route I take, it strikes me the sun is part
me, part the start of day, the birds and weeds,
part the far green hill, the other side where I'm
trying to go, part stars at night high overhead,
bright and far, part dark as well.   I'm thin

of light sometimes. I think so dimly
my eyes wish – they wish to open. Then
when I least expect it, when my hideout's done
I wake and it's not even morning. It's five
in the afternoon, quarter past, and there's work
to do. It's seven eight, eleven at night, and
what I see is as beautiful as, what I see is immensely
our universe, only closer – the hour I'm home.

I'd love to greet you. Here I am. Dust on the floor,
spider resting on my shoe, last hour this day.
The world is quiet, the music shy, the lean
I do against the wall. All life begins to breathe,
all light to listen. Who can I tell what I see? I see
you every option, you every tree dizzying breeze,
every bit of heat, every fraction and word, each
one who comes by, the fire of matches, the
first of all roads and that faint fleet star. How
could I ever not, when I close my eyes,
when open and home, deep in arms, when
the dark's outdoors, how not live
with you, not know your face

Longing For Space

Forever has no meaning in the light
of human ties. There is us, there is our,
every you of me, and no time
that wedges its way between. Only love

longing for space.   Life on earth –
mud on the shore, crisis of restlessness,
trees in the wind. Very little air that's not
taken up. A boatload of travelers
trying to get home. I have learned
to appreciate how we each also long
to discover our soul.   Here

the sun sings early and lateness speaks
when the stars are out. I look across the water,
encouraged not to sleep. The call
of a coyote this summer night.
What I see is a step to take. Coming closer to all

life

After A Long Rain

Walked down to meet the spring the flowering trees
the bird in the puddle splashed my soul, took off
even though I wanted it to stay, I wanted
the robin the worms didn't want it, I did. Couldn't

keep anything in place, not the wind, the dripping leaves.
Three swallows flew past. Quick the chipmunk. Nothing
stays put, I thought. All I hoped for was to talk. The sun
burst from behind the low clouds. I'm here, I said. Here.

It takes time to get to know someone. To let
their inside be your inside and your inside be theirs.
The sun did not say this to me, it sprang it sang
light to spark the fresh birch leaves, evening light, shadows

on the ground, light going down, rising in me after so much hiding,
bright through my body, my breathing thoughts, each growing word. May I walk
with you? asked the light. I have come to your soil to your soul. I can't
do it without you. Sure, sun. Sure, I said. You can walk with me

always. I watched as the sun disappeared behind the hill. Soon
I'd welcome the darkness. Light of the darkness. I lingered. Felt
a gust of wind to follow – the universe I am, each person I'm not,
birds stones puddles to speak with. From the inside out. Let's go

The Nature Of Light

The nature of light is not seen. Or it is seen
in my inability to see it. That or I am unable
only because I look the wrong way – far
at the sun, as if it's an object for analysis

when I should hold it in my heart, a caretaker
of life. But maybe I'm being too hard
on myself. Soften, I say when I know
I am listening. And I fill with light

THE SOUL TREE

There are days I think I see the soul. Tree
in these quiet woods, people in my life. I
talked to a woman whose child had died.

She stood next to me and the sun
upon the side of her face kept bright
watch. The other side hidden. Her words

full of light encouraged me to follow
the path of reality. I didn't take it on.
I told her, I'm sorry. And she said, *Don't be*

sorry. Be yourself. Even better, be the sun
how it brings courage every day
where its words inside you burst forth

from behind the clouds. Like pulling splinters
from the heart, be free of what prevents you. Think
what you have not thought before, love

all life that gives you its looks. The tree
we're standing under is a birch.
I looked up, and so it was

The Chance To Be Visible

I stand in the corner of all that I am
thinking feeling knowing there's more
to me than the floor I'm on, the problem walls.
Around me are windows, doors I don't yet see.

There are stars, stairs in the sky, hidden by blue. And days
of my destiny in the riddling world. Who can answer
how everything is woven? It's a generous knit
whose color is ours, if ours is a fox

 a stone, a green conversation. I don't really know. I
see colors everywhere, though. They come in
boxes with ribbons, and in the rainbow that follows
an afternoon shower, painting itself upon

the dark grey clouds, the sun breaking free.   Free.   Free
at last. We are caught in the web of this world, and life
doesn't flinch. It stands alongside, urging us
out of corners, from the inside out, for

whatever we are meant to be. What is it, unless
unclouded, included, a source of light? My story
turns emptiness into interest. Attention on trees, peace
in the palm, the bluest of all birds, a most delicious

bread offered to you. I am this place
spun for love, as if love could spin, not a tale
to keep me cornered or stuck, but the chance
to be visible in what moves I make

The Change

Nothing will change
until we change and
we will not change
until we understand why
we live and why we die.
We live to transform ourselves.
And we die to realize
the greater life
of one another.

Around us, the earth
is made of greater life. Green
leaves. Brown eyes. Loud
thunder. Undulating
existence. We are made
of earth and others, too. And we will not see
the others in ourselves
until we see each other
in the world around.   You

are not invisible, you
have my attention, you
comprise the body and soul, the being
before me, beautiful
as a tree a butterfly a stone. I

wake each morning on earth. I move
together with you, seeing no longer
the littleness of self-interests
the frets and fears and cravings
but rather the opening
of my eyes upon my heart. My mind
takes in all that forms me
so that I may become mountains, streets
rainfall – the world I live in. You and I

belong in this place, upon
the unimpeded path of becoming
ourselves, not a dream but
the enduring route of human
wakefulness, none of it
deferred, none
of it shackled, no one
deemed less valuable, neither
belittled nor consumed. O

the earth sails on, spins
our home through space. The sun
sheds light with its love, shares
its days with us. The way I see it
light fills me with the beauty
of everything, everyone. And each moment
I may welcome it. Sometimes
I'm a bucket, other times
an umbrella. A bench by the stream
one day, and the next
a closed door. And I know
nothing will change
until I do

The Reason

Morning stillness   I too
am still   silent
as the snow   that mutes
the land   that coats
the trees   renews
each path   with possibilities.
No easy wind   knocks
the winter door.   I hear
hardships   deep drifts
the urgent day   the hail
of light   I can't
      hold still
I have to   move
transform with life. And love
 – the reason I am here –
can only   be born
in the world   through me

About the Author

Leif Garbisch is a writer and photographer who, with his wife, Kerry, divides his time between Sarasota, Florida and Ghent, New York. In Florida there are three amazing granddaughters and many alligators, while in New York there are trees that change colors in autumn and a quality of light that is more satisfying and interesting. Garbisch has published several novels, including *Conduit*, *The Shore*, and *The Magic Us*, as well as six books containing his photographs and poetry. He is currently completing a novel tentatively entitled, *Move*.

www.ingramcontent.com/pod-product-compliance
Lightning Source LLC
Chambersburg PA
CBHW081159070526
44583CB00021B/2907